Till värld

Allt gott i världen ov...

GH00889025

MINDFLOSSING

100% PURE FROM CONCENTRATE

Harvested By

JAKOB WAHLBERG

- ➢ Cover design by Jakob Wahlberg.

- ➢ "The Train Ride – A Mother's Tale" written by Birgitta Lennerstrand. Edited by Jakob Wahlberg.

- ➢ All photographs by Jakob Wahlberg and Birgitta Lennerstrand.

authorHOUSE™

1663 LIBERTY DRIVE, SUITE 200
BLOOMINGTON, INDIANA 47403
(800) 839-8640
WWW.AUTHORHOUSE.COM

First published by AuthorHouse 2/1/2006

ISBN: 1-4259-0346-0 (sc)

Library of Congress Control Number: 2005910771

Printed in the United States of America
Bloomington, Indiana

This book is printed on acid-free paper.

"Imagination is more important than knowledge. For knowledge is limited, whereas imagination embraces the entire world, stimulating progress, giving birth to evolution."

— **Albert Einstein**

TABLE OF CONTENTS

FOREWORD

For some time, I've been thinking about how to capture thoughts and impressions about life experiences that are a part of my internal self. A couple of years ago, I started writing some of these things down simply because I enjoyed it and to save whatever sanity that I had left. Shortly thereafter, when I ran out of sanity, I started digging in the rubble that remained, discovering what was actually present. The result of those "mind-flossing attempts" is this book.

Big thanks for the feedback to:
Rick Maier, Kathryn Colburn, Dinnie McLaughlin, Clarice Navish, Jennifer Cataldo, and Elizabeth Wallace.

Special thanks to:
Birgitta Lennerstrand, Per-Arne Björklund, Agneta Wahlberg, Fredrik and Inger Wahlberg with family, Lee and Frances Burris, in spirit Mormor Astrid and Majsan, and everyone involved at AuthorHouse.

Very special thanks to Joyce Wahlberg for all her invaluable help, feedback, and inspiration.

This book is dedicated in very loving memory to my dad, Axel Wahlberg.

WHAT PEOPLE HAVEN'T SAID ABOUT THE BOOK...YET...

"He must be an alien..."

"It cured my diabetes!"

"Oh dear... I need a stiff drink... make it a double!"

"I lost 250 pounds in ten days!"

"Huh? I don't get it..."

"I don't have time for this &#%@!!!"

"Life's too short — who needs introspective?"

"My hair grew back!!!"

"I bathe and go to bed with it every day..."

"Who knew he had this inside him? His therapist?"

"He really sounds like high maintenance..."

"I'm not sure if my level of honesty can accept these concepts..."

"Pure Mind Lotion!"

AMBIVALENT

You stand there, suddenly completely empty.
All thoughts spinning, nothing sticks. The wheel
spins faster, the flame intensifies.

Stress is climbing on you and consciously kicks
you in the stomach. Oh God, what am I going to
do?

Have to do the right thing...must find...must
choose...Must.

Why isn't anybody helping me? Can't they see
what a hard time I'm having?

Right...left...up...down...high...low...a lot...a little.

Damn, the clouds are low!

Black and white. Drastic. Nothing in between.
Must...hard...soft...Must.

1

Somebody, help me!

No eye contact — everybody's looking away.
Invisible in the crowd — alone in my mess.

Long line behind me.
Guilty.
Too many choices.
Embarrassed.
Must.
Must now.

- A medium cup of chocolate-vanilla swirl,
please...

BAD PRODUCT IDEAS

Brownie Paper Towels
Eat your own mess!

Celebration H
Hemorrhoid cream for when it is going away

Blasterine Mouth Rinse
Kill whatever is alive in your mouth

Golgate Toothpaste
Crucify your tartar!

Tuneafish
The Musical Seafood

AZ Gel
Formerly in KY

The Catalytic Church
Run by the Pipe

No Wonder Bread
More insight by the slice

Of Coors Light Beer
Naturally your choice!

Booty Bread
Enjoy our varieties "Rumpernickel", "Dark Rye of the Moon" and "Crack'n Oat Bran"

Coca Koala
Australian Soda

Shampoopoo
For really "pooey" hair

Salmon
The Other Pink Meat

ABBU
Middle Eastern pop group

Einstein's Cloning Juice
Make your own Zweistein or Threestein

Risin' Bran
Cereal Viagra

Liesol
Clean up the evidence

Duncan Donuts
Get your Scottish haggis éclair here!

Vibrated Moo
Alternative Milk Shake

Pimp Tarts Candy
Now with Ho Wheat!

Bubble Gump
Forrest Flavor

Ice Cream Fudge Tuesday
Cure the early week blues

Soap Operetta
Lighter daytime conspiracies

XL Files
Extra-large adventures with agents Éclair and McNugget

The Buyble
Shopping Guide for the Faithful

The Olympig Games
Buffet competition for serious eaters

The Vagina Dialogues
Part Two of the Monologues

The Ten Condiments
The sweet truth delivered at Mountain Dew

Ben-Hurl
Bulimic gladiator toy

Blitz Serenity
German relaxation kit

BLAH BLAH BLAH

Inside, a rainbow of feelings, but no display.
Inside, an ocean of tears, with nowhere to go.
Inside, a heart so heavy, earth would shatter.

You say you listen, but you don't hear my words.

You say you see, but you're not looking.

You say you promise, but you don't follow
through.

You say you care, but on your terms only.

You say you will, but you really won't.

You say a lot, but only deliver more
nothingness...

CHAMELEON MARATHON

Flip flop, back forth, up down, left right,
forward backward, in out, white black,
hot cold, a little a lot, light dark, spicy mild,
present absent, detached involved, here there,
nowhere everywhere, neutrally opinionated,
calmly hyperventilating.

A solid transparent.

All roads lead to somewhere, but border to
nowhere.

Who are you?
What is real?

All of it.

CHAT WITH EINSTEIN'S DRUNKEN GHOST

During a séance session, a medium accidentally summoned the wrong spirit. Instead of the intended relative, the intoxicated ghost of Albert Einstein appeared. Since the situation was rather unique, despite its "mistake," the people present wanted to seize the moment and communicate with the brilliant scientist on the other side. The following is a transcript of the session as it was communicated via chat software on a computer.

Q: Hey, which came first — the chicken or the egg?
AE: The chicken had the first orgasm. LOL!

Q: Which fuel do you prefer — gasoline or ethanol?
AE: I would pass the gas and head straight for the alcohol.

Q: Boxers or briefs?
AE: Not into violent sports or short meetings.

Q: You once wrote "Great spirits have always encountered violent opposition from mediocre minds." What exactly did you mean by that statement?
AE: To Hell with dry counties! ☺

Q: How would you describe yourself in twenty-five words or less?
AE: Hey...how old did you say your name was...wazzup...wanna do now...bork bork bork...another beer! LOL! How many was that?

Q: Is there a side of yourself that you didn't know existed until you started writing?
AE: Carpal Tunnel Syndrome.

Q: Who is your biggest influence today?
AE: Homer Simpson.

Q: If you could choose anyone to write your biography, who would it be?
AE: Malcolm McLaren, who managed the Sex Pistols. Brilliant!

Q: What piece of advice would you give to aspiring scientists?
AE: Don't eat beans and work near a Bunsen burner.

Q: What is your favorite vegetable?
AE: Beer nuts.

Q: What is your favorite food?
AE: Harry Potter's "Spaghetti and Meat Sorcerer."

Q: What is your favorite drink?
AE: Harvey Wallbanger!

Q: What is your favorite movie?
AE: "Smokey and the Buddhist" starring Burt Reynolds and The Dalai Lama.

Q: If you were stranded on a deserted island, what items would you bring?
AE: A micro brewery, crackers, and government cheese.

Q: What color is your hair?
AE: Confused chaos with a touch of rhubarb.

Q: Poultry or seafood?
AE: Flying fish.

Q: What do you think about reality TV?
AE: It's about as real as processed cheese but might taste ok if served right.

Q: Who would you want as president of the United States?

AE: Well, since Gandhi is dead, I would have to say Conan O'Brien.

Q: If you could be an animal, which one would it be?
AE: A red-footed Booby bird.

Q: What's the best book you have ever read?
AE: Lord of the Onion Rings. Love the "Friedough" character!

Q: How important is a formal education?
AE: It's vital to learn, but I refuse to accept a diploma on a wall as anything else other than evidence of acceptable attendance plus proof of purchase.

Q: Describe three wishes of yours!
AE: I want to order meats at the deli counter in British stones, give directions using a combined version of miles and kilometers divided by three, plus buy gas by the pint.

Q: How can women learn more about men?
AE: Use a "dicktionary" and look it up. Kidding!

Q: What do you think about fashion?
AE: I have always refused to be in style. I will do as I please, and if the end result adds any attractive aspects to my physical being, so be it.

Q: How important is freedom of speech?
AE: I will always fully support freedom of speech, but would like to append social responsibility and respect to the amendment. Now be quiet! LOL!

Q: What ticks you off?
AE: Hmm...tail-hangers, followers and cowards, country music gives me a bad rash, selfish people with "Opera Singer Syndrome" (me-me-me-me-me), Julia Louis-Dreyfus's hairstyle in *Seinfeld*, coffee or tea served cold, and bad salami.

Q: What makes you happy?
AE: Doggies! Human life would be so much less complicated if we all had tails and their positive spirit!

Q: What is your all-time favorite TV show?
AE: It's a combination of three: *The Simpsons, Monty Python's Flying Circus,* and *The Muppet Show.*

Q: Any parting thoughts for the remaining living?
AE: Go Red Sox! Go Pats! Bork Bork Bork! Ni! Doh! Bottoms up! Allrightythen! Oh, and thank God for L'Oreal products — I'm *finally* worth something! LOL!

Later, ya'll... ☺

P.S.: E=MC Hammer!

CLICHÉ EDITORIAL

"Always look on the bright side of life."
- What's wrong with the shade?

"You live and learn."
- So you can learn to live?

"Shit happens."
- And for those it doesn't happen to, there are laxatives.

"What goes around, comes around."
- Not if you cripple it first!

"Don't worry, be happy!"
- Share whatever you're on, please!

"Laughter is the best medicine."
- After pain-killers and alcohol.

"Same shit, different day."

- See your doctor; something is not right with your plumbing!

"Smile...it makes people wonder."
- Sure, like what kind of nutjob you are!

"There is harmony in disharmony."
- That would explain Bob Dylan.

"Tomorrow is another day."
- For screwing everything up again!

"Every cloud has a silver lining."
- Made out of lead from global pollution.

"There is a light at the end of the tunnel."
- ...that needs a new bulb.

"This, too, shall pass."
- ...said the idiot who had swallowed a brick.

"Life's not so bad, when you consider the alternative."
- What alternative? The other *better* life?

"The darker the berry, the sweeter the wine."
- What about the case of Chateau Dingle?

"All good things come to those who wait."
- How to reduce active competitors.

"Zero is sometimes better than nothing."

- Hi! I failed math!

"One day, I will wake up, and it will all fit together."
- The miracles of duct tape.

"Time will tell."
- Please stop telling Time; it can't keep its mouth shut!

"Someday, my ship will come in."
- Until then: Row, you little bastard! Row!

"When in doubt, consult your inner child."
- This just in: An adult has been charged with three counts of inner child abuse. "The little &#^%$ just wouldn't shut the #*&%@ up!"

"If it doesn't come naturally, leave it."
- Enter Viagra.

"Indecision is the key to flexibility."
- The Procrastinator Bible, Chapter 1, Verse 1.

"Life is not hard; it only needs some positive thinking."
- You forgot drugs.

"Life is a bitch."
- Say hi to Life, the female canine.

"When God gives you lemons, make lemonade."

- ...and add VODKA!

"Never forget that you are unique, just like everybody else."
- If you're just like everybody else, how can you be unique? Had you said "eunuch," I would continue listening...

"You can win by not losing."
- Hey, dass really schmart!!!

"The meek shall inherit the earth."
- After it has been violated by Klingons...

"It is the inside that really matters."
- Sure, just like the articles in *Playboy* magazine.

"Beauty is a matter of taste."
- Then taste is a matter of buds — therefore, having a Bud is a beautiful thing!

"Beauty is only skin deep."
- And then you start peeling...

"Beauty is in the eye of the beholder."
- Well, get Beauty out of Beholder's eye!

"You can't tell a book by its cover."
- Fire the cover designer now!

"It's only fear that makes you run."
- Nope, undercooked chicken does too.

"No guts, no glory."
- Haggis: food for glorious people.

"There is nothing to fear but fear itself."
- Plus the fear of that!

"I just followed my intuition."
- ...and the voices of pink elephants.

"Sorry, I did not mean to hurt you."
- I was just thinking 100% about myself.

"Nobody is perfect."
- I'm a nobody, so I must be perfect!

"I'm only human."
- Hey, stop it! It *is* your fault!

"It seemed like a good idea at the time."
- When you are above posted warning signs.

"When at first you don't succeed, try again."
- And you will succeed at failing again!

"Rome was not built in a day."
- They're still not done, are they?

"If at first you don't succeed, redefine success."
- Anyone can be a winner in moral mayhem.

CONCEIT

Vanity's amplification of portions of the natural self that one cannot feel. No batteries required.

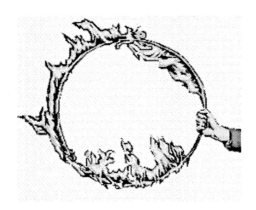

DARE

I look at you and see nothingness. Wondering if
simplicity or ignorance rules. A shell alive but
without a sense of self. Taking in but not giving,
a continuous motion.

I wonder if you really know what is around you.
If you understand what actually hits you. Trained
responses make a smooth performance. Stand
for nothing. Don't offend.

What are you hiding that is so important? What
are you scared of that is so big? Or maybe, you
simply don't care or understand. Your universe is
big enough.

Sometimes, I envy the shallow, weak, and cold.
Life is so much simpler with little or nothing
to reach. You can close your eyes and sleep in

nothingness. Dream of secrets you comfortably
never will expose.

Selfish happiness motivates the chosen path.
Aim at achievable targets not to disappoint.
Everything is according to plan, rail has been
laid. Secure, can't miss target even if you tried.

Nothingness can grow, populate, and infect.
A condition due to fear and missing sense of
purpose. Sensors present but turned off, filters
rule. Until you wake up, missing and regretting.

Awareness hurts, but it is what makes you a
bigger person. If you want to be.

If you dare.

DETACHED ATTACHMENT

A longing for something you have always wanted but can never have. What is left from the emotional yearning is a logical reality. A strong solidarity to the efforts put in. It is something to hold on to compared to many speculative what-ifs.

But, you are still feeling empty and a bit cheated. Did I do something wrong? Have I really done all I can? Is there something wrong with me?

I wonder if what we really want actually exists anywhere but as a notion in our heart.

DOWNLOAD ME

Wireless.
Internet.
E-mail.
Chat room.
Fax.
SMS.
A personal beacon.
Connected.

We exist more.
We talk about nothing.
We kill time.
We download distractions.
We pose using other identities.
We hide who we are.
We feel even lonelier if not contacted.
We lose touch with ourselves using amazing
means of communication.
Disconnected.

Go figure.

DUEL

Emotion and Logic stand with their weapons drawn. The immediate showdown is inevitable.

The spectators are quickly gathering.

Love is holding Insecurity's hand and whispers comforting words.

Determination stands alone and worried.

Self-confidence doesn't know where to stand to see what happens.

Fear is hiding behind a shadow.

Ego stands in front of everyone and blocks the view.

Intellect scratches its head due to lack of stimulation.

Need is fighting for space with Ego.

Sexuality couldn't come.

Intuition and Insight look bored since the outcome already is predicted.

Impatience bites its nails and tickles Stimulation to distract.

Surface looks away at something else.

The hour falls.
Two shots fired.
Both hit.
A decision has been made.

He will apologize to her...

ENTITLEMENT

The Ego's instinctive attempt to heal its open wounds with Band-Aids created by the needs of the moment...because it's always your turn.

erogeNOuS zonE

What if the nose was the most erogenous zone for men and women?

Being "nosy" would be a sexual compliment. To blow your nose would be considered masturbation. Every sneeze, an orgasm. Hay fever and allergies — you lucky dog!

Would a big nose be favorable? Would "brown nosing" be equivalent to asking for sexual favors? Would picking your nose finally become sensual? Would a clown nose call a different kind of attention?

Would hairy noses suddenly become sexy? Victoria's Secret would only sell handkerchiefs and nasal spray. Would people start snorting pepper instead of cocaine? Would calling in sick due to a cold be legitimate or would you be considered a pervert?

Would eyewear designers create new products that would stimulate while wearing them? Would plastic surgery primarily be done for performance enhancements?

Would animals with prominent nasal features be the favorite pets to have? Would *Rudolph the Red-nosed Reindeer* be given an "R" rating?

Would odors be a kind of foreplay? Would a clothespin on your nose be considered kinky? Boxing would be outlawed due to the risk of sexual side effects. To "put your nose where it doesn't belong" would be sexual harassment.

The actual "size" would never be a mystery to either men or women. Since you would see a pleasure zone everywhere you looked — would it make people happier? No more embarrassing "shrinkage problems" in colder temperatures.

You would not get pregnant with unwanted kids. Some people would still fake orgasms. And finally, would people be able to tell if you were horny?

FAITH

With an open, objective mind and without any burden of scientific proof, having the courage to allow things you don't fully understand to affect you because they feel right.

FIRST TIME

You will never forget the first time you saw it. You carefully touched it, slowly moving your fingers up and down. You knew right away you wanted to.

When you felt more comfortable, you got enough courage to try. You grabbed a hold of it and slowly put it in between your legs. You held on tight with both hands when you slowly sat down on top of it. You felt a tingling sensation of being in control.

Since it's the first time, he's holding onto you for support. After a while, he lets go. A little wobbly at first but you soon return to the pumping rhythm. I can! I can!

You'll never forget the first bike ride.

FLOCK DISEASE

In flocks, I feel the most alone. Can't relate to masses. A lump sum too big for comfort, leaving me restless and agitated.

I see nothing wrong with others choosing to join a flock. After all, you will have company and you may find valuable purpose spending your care on similar or needing others.

Flock people mostly produce collective things. They get valuable strength from mass energy. Voids are filled in a place of solidarity and belonging, where "you" are wanted. All you have to do is to fit in and don't stick out too much.

Majority may rule in some cases, all for good and well. But, some flocks act like a narcissistic swinger party where you become a nutrition-based member in a quilted collective. Your identity, a part of a big pattern that will be fed to many to reinforce, stimulate and ultimately control.

In flocks, I can't shake the feeling of dissolving, melting like an Amazon snowman. Maybe that's what one has to do in order to fit in? Liquid can easily be reshaped compared to solid matters.

Liquid usually leaves an irregular trail of its presence and path. People leave footprints — a stamp of one's presence and sense of origin. Like sandcastles on the beach, liquid can wash them away. The funny thing is when mixing liquid and sand a certain way, one can produce concrete.

When searching for a sense of belonging, one can feel even more alone if in the wrong company. A reminder of loneliness in a group setting can be very powerful, yet quite ironic too.

FORGIVENESS

As Love's cornerstone, an acceptance, release, and absolution based on a desire to heal and evolve.

A place where you are bigger than the issue.

Where the path to change begins.

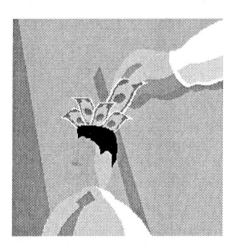

GREED

The carried-out testament of human garbage.

GROWING PEACEFUL

The unconditional acceptance and realization of universal and constant transition.

To be at peace with not having all the answers and to stay in motion.

A surrender to what actually is, identifying what isn't, and collectively become one in mind and spirit.

HANG ON

Eyes wide open, the impact still warm.
Awake in humility, lost in meaning.
Starting fires with past flames.
Unresolved ashes remain.

Smearing my colors, fingers tripping.
My clay is hardening, soon too late to shape.
Chaos raging, a tornado wild.
Fractional reality, little grip.

An action dilemma, the choice of battles.
Voices many but no solid choir.
A performance of restraint, Oscar-worthy.
Rewire the detonator for another day.

HAPPINESS

An internal agreement of path, purpose, and self-awareness — producing peace and space for joy to exist.

HELLO

Confuse.
Discredit.
Contradict.
Shock.

Amaze.
Revoke.
Spew.
Withhold.

Mislead.
Offend.
Deny.
Propagate.

A self-made freak machine running at 1,000 RPM.
Desperately patching emptiness with opposites.
Can't affect what is already torn, gaps too wide.

Nobody will know you but you will be noticed.

HOPE

I wonder sometimes if desires color the retina
so reality appears more attractive. Elaborate
dreams embellish but not for long. The constant
journey from chaos to cosmos — when will the
soul get to rest? The image in the mirror needs
to clear up.

We look for answers and guidance. Try to
make a new costume with the internal red
thread. Patterns many — but few pieces fit well
together. Which is right? Can one be irregular
with the universe and still have a place?

We have a need to believe but are not sure how to handle logical limits. Feeling the draft from the open doors.

A buffering layer between opposite forces — unable to be shaped to fit. Many appear to have discovered — but how?

Coincidences lack validity.

One has to be lucky, though. Need at least one bulls-eye to feel one's center.

Jakob Wahlberg

HOW DOES IT FEEL?

One way to truly relate to other people's feelings
is to look at them through the eyes of your own
vulnerability.

I WILL

For Wisdom, I will live.
For Convenience, I will pay.
For Hatred, I will suffer.
For Struggle, I will conquer.
For Truth, I will seek.
For Clarity, I will challenge.
For Injustice, I will fight.
For Love, I will surrender.

I will, therefore I shall.

IF YOU ONLY KNEW

If your internal thought process was verbalized, would your friends still say they know you?

INVISIBLE

I stand erect without being reflected on any retina. My voice carries without receivers. I aim my care at moving targets. The lack of precision reduces the intended effect.

My generosity, often taken. I explain but few relate. I receive roots of nothingness. Emptiness, a growing infestation.

My flame needs a new wick. Abilities, but no real happiness. Options, but no path. My internal puzzle, an irregular motif.

A lesson in progress, difficult to accept. Outside the box, where I feel at home.

I am...but invisible.

LIMBO INN

Welcome to the Limbo Inn!

We are conveniently located in the state of Confinement.

All guest rooms and suites are equipped with automatic Toss-and-Turn technology beds.

All TV programs offered on our internal cable system are from the '70s and in all-day-marathon format. We also offer an endless supply of infomercials where you can purchase widgets, gadgets, and toys to pass time with.

Instead of the Internet, we offer you to use our own "Internot" — a network of everything that simply isn't. Our internal search engine can be found at yawho://doink/deadend.

Our very own phone service, Ze Phöne, is available in every room or "cell" as we call them. To assist you with your time-passing needs, we have rewired all extensions to a Random Connection Generator, so your guess is as good as ours where your cell call may end up. This will keep you busy for a while — you have our word on it.

Our fax service, FLUX, will send all your faxes to the Oblivion data center. Naturally, your originals will be "eaten" accordingly by the machine at the end of each transmission and there will be no available records of any attempts to send anything.

Our twenty-four-hour gym facility has the latest hamster-wheel and dead-weight technology. You will also have access to an endless supply of water to tread in our luxurious indoor pool and spa. We have a designated section for surface people in the shallow end of the pool.

Visit our famous hiking trails, located somewhere around our establishment, where everyone takes two steps forward and one step back — guaranteed.

And for the kids, we have an endless supply of interactive toys as well as "Super Maze" — a never-ending labyrinth that will keep the little ones (or adults) busy for as long as you like. Don't worry — we haven't lost anyone permanently in there yet!

For a pleasant dining experience in a relaxing environment, we highly recommend our own "Halfway House," located in the lobby of the Limbo Inn. From an All-U-Can-Eat buffet to a plethora of other choices, we cater to your needs, whatever they may be. In the interest of passing time, our wait staff will read all 648 menu items out loud before taking your order.

Feel like dancing? Why not participate in some limbo dancing — available every night in our Forever Velvet nightclub!

We also offer many workshops to suit your taste. "Make your own unsolvable puzzle," "Time Perception — make one minute last a lifetime," "Mathematic Theorems 101," "Make it last longer — What we can learn from Bureaucracy Theory," just to name a few.

Our Lost and Found department is open daily on a randomly selected and unadvertised schedule.

Our complimentary shuttle service will pick you up and drop you off whenever you like. Please note that the drop-off destinations may vary and change at a moment's notice. Don't worry — you'll get "somewhere" most of the time.

Special indefinite booking packages are available from Whenever to Forever.

We accept all major credit cards, including American Slowness, SlaveCard and Miner's Club.

As an involuntary but valued guest, we will do everything we can to ensure you will enjoy your stagnant stay with us!

For more information and reservations, please visit our Web site at w3.internet.not/limboinn.

Sincerely,

The Limbo Inn Management

LOST IN A NEW BEGINNING

A heart in pieces, reasons many. Emotions, a prosecutor hunting crimes. So many signs, all pointing in different directions. Scared to admit, have so little left to lose.

Attack to understand, but logic is failing. Blindness frightens, what is possibly missed again. What is too big to overcome can be broken down. Must connect the many pieces, one picture united.

What is so precious, if protected with a lie? What is so important if allowed to slowly die? Staring at answers, sometimes don't want to see. A different path needed, away.

To put on hold what the heart finds sacred —

a punishment as well as a crime. A prisoner, convicted of lost time. The window of freedom, bars in deep.

So sorry for the sins, guilty with a stained conscience. Asking for forgiveness, difficult to receive. An awakening after almost all is lost. Why hold on to what will ultimately desert you?

A hostage, ransom changed daily. Forcing submission, controlled by convictions. I'm living pieces others choose to ignore. Want so badly to be different, to impact what I touch.

My fire is flickering, pain dulls the flame. Produce hope, but faith is weakening. Hanging onto something, roots unknown. Searching for connections, little energy returned.

Life is at the door, need to invite it. Want to be a bigger person than issues at hand. Newborn clarity, the guide to my universe.

The whipping winds of ambition, never settle. I am a host of an internal hurricane. But you will never see the path of its wrath.

I hope to end up where the circle completes.

MENTOR IN THE SKY

The calmness of the clouds' slow dance speaks
to my soul. Without worry, just float around
and be admired for its beauty. Regardless of the
direction of the wind, they securely go along.

If two separate airstreams meet, important
nutrients are produced for the vegetation below.
What if we humans could work like that: Just
to harmonically meet and naturally produce
something important, without even trying.

We humans are fairly unlike the clouds. We often
cover what makes us feel good. Our emotions
flash uncomfortably in our soul. Bad memories
don't always blow away with time.

The clouds are very different from us in one
way: they are always clouds. They are not trying

to be anything else. They exist where they are and allow what happens to happen, naturally.

It doesn't matter to the clouds if they are thin or thick, white or colored. It's a real family with room for everyone. Maybe this Mentor in the Sky is there as inspiration to us humans.

If you were a cloud, what would the sky look like then?

MY NOW

My thoughts, a collected, focused present.
My touch, one sincere meaning.
My kiss, past and future attached.
My moment, a sincere immediacy.

You get all there is.
Here and now.
Always.

ODE TO SIMPLICITY

All the walls came down, a melting man of snow. Knowing now they had to, a recovery from low. No more protecting what needs to grow in peace. No more pretending, no more show to please.

I can't go back to what used to be. I need to finally set all of me free. I want to allow my passion to get out from its box. It has been very lonely, hidden behind many locks.

I've been searching for answers in many a place. All this time, it has been staring me in the face. I try to take comfort in possibilities ahead. Wondering where it will take me, thinking, lying on my bed.

I want to enjoy the simple and reduce the complexity. I want to appreciate what is truly me. While shadows may be lurking and some ghosts may appear, I have started a new direction that will take me out of here.

Allow the process to become gold from a wishing well. Allow all the roads ahead to point away from where I fell. See the simple beauty and appreciate its glow. Stop and smell the roses and go with the flow.

My ode to Simplicity is a wish for every man who is genuinely trying to be as happy as he can. While I may not have the answer to what sets us all apart, my wish is to bring us closer, living from the heart.

ON MY RETINA

As I exit, images and words are forever stored
in my heart's most sacred vault. I carry this
treasure and guard it with my every breath.

A final cadence in progress. A fighter's will,
defying the odds. An unfair fight, an unworthy
ending. An ultimate injustice, greeted by doubt.
A godly absence. A prolonged surrender.

In all this darkness, you are a beacon. Your glow,
carried forward by many. Your reach, far and
beyond. Your presence, a gift and unerasable
footprint.

How I will miss you, no words will ever be
enough. All the things unspoken, now left
in petty peace. A surrender to a worthy
understanding.

As the door is closing, everything turns into slow-
motion. Your back already turned, head down,
slowly walking away. A giant disguised in a baby
bird's clothing. This may very well be the last
time we witnessed each other's pulse. Difficult
to fully appreciate the blessing — so much rage
over a punishment without a crime.

I've done and said everything I can think of. I
hope you know that. But is it enough? I remind
myself that you may not want some of it because
of the attached attention to the sad matter. It
might seem selfish but these thoughts have to
exit — I'm sorry — can't keep them inside.

So, I guess I'll write it all down.
Here you go.
With love.
Always.

ONE — SORT OF...

Parents.
Memories.
Experiences.
Feelings.
Friends.
Opinions.
Standards.
Judgments.
Impressions.
Choices.
Paths.

So many multiples.

We are supposed to be *one* of a kind.

How does one differentiate from being an individual or a collection?

Does it really matter?

ONE SECOND

It is now. It was then.

The world is changing with ticking beats. Now becomes then, again and again. The heart of the day, a pulse that never stops. Everything calculated. Everything predictable.

It is now. It was then.

Why is the present so short? How can we have time to enjoy when what is, suddenly was? Is the second too short to be appreciated? Do memories mean more since they seem longer?

I just thought that.

PEA BRAIN

Your mere existence is a chemical mystery. Unlike insects, you simply exist and cannot be used as food for anyone. You have no function — only consume valuable oxygen that should go to others with a purpose.

The glass walls in your soul are fragile and foggy. The surface — the only acceptable level. When you occasionally open the flood gates to your ill logic, you frighten what is around you.

You are desperately holding onto the People's Tail. Can only exist in resemblance of others. To prove your existence, you must mark all of your territory — whether it belongs to you or not.

Conflict is another evidence of your pathetic existence and you choose to provoke to get attention. Alone, you're nothing — existing only as a reflection of your surroundings' reactions.

Who are you, really?

You are like expired potting soil with no nutrition left. It's impossible to punish a non-addable zero like yourself. Your worst punishment is to be who you are.

Meow.

PERSONAL AD RECIPE

Woman Wanted
- Low Fat
- Two ripe melons
- Juicy Rump Roast
- Smooth Legs of Lamb
- No nutcracker
- Not smoked
- No bun in the oven
- No eggs in the basket
- Sweet without calories

Man Wanted
- Non fat
- Natural (not a Boar)
- Authentic Soup-to-Nuts
- No Meat head
- A real King Salami
- A bag of fresh nuts
- Bologna free
- No chicken
- No flakes

PRESENT PAST

Once upon a time will never be again.

The past, a forever-changing memory. The recollection less accurate with time, flavored by life.

Sometimes reshaped, a relationship renewed. With subjective accuracy, a modified past to fit into a forever-changing present.

The difference between truth and fiction, sometimes hair thin.

RAGE

A lack of self-containment when one's emotional boundaries are stretched beyond manageability. A human volcano, erupting emotional lava.

RIDDLE

To figure out the truth behind what you need to hear yourself say.

$&M.CON

Dear Neighbor,

We are writing you today to introduce ourselves with an offer you can't refuse: *Get the Real Deal!*

Prior to writing this letter, we injected ourselves with 2,000 mg of truth serum so you can bet your bottom dollar that what you are about to read below is the whole truth (plus the added incentive of a court order telling us we had to do it). Here are the details of "The Real Deal" (in no particular order):

We will lubricate your frail minds so we can thrust our marketing tools into you. You're already so full of fear and doubt, it's easy to attack your weaknesses. In order for us to own you and your business, we will use any means possible to get our message across. For example (but not limited to):

We will make chickens parade. Despite being slaughtered and headless, they will dance for you to appeal to your primitive taste buds. Mmmmm, looks soooooo tasty!!!

We will have bears jump around with joy since there's now a softer and more absorbent toilet paper. We know that you trust the bear's judgment. If it works for wiping their behinds — it will certainly work for you!

We will make junk food dance — so you can ingest instant happiness and have true "fun" while getting fatter and more depressed.

We will give you a pill to remedy every pain — you "are" suffering from something, aren't you?

We will defy science and make animals talk, sing, and dance for you. Hey, we *are* that good and we don't have to pay union scale to actors!

We will stereotype and use clichés so you can relate — you're too frigging dumb to get our message otherwise.

We will offer you to buy two and pay for three — if we say it's a great deal, it frigging is.

We will sell pure products from concentrate — they are "pure $" to us.

We will offer you beauty products for restoring lost youth. None of them *really* works for more than thirty minutes, but we want to express our sincerest thanks to our most valued customer: your vanity.

We will add subliminal messages in our ads. We've done our homework — we know you better than yourself.

We will only disclose the *actual* details of a deal in flashing, illegible fine print — decryption code, special glasses and legal education required to read.

We will whip up fifty-nine artificial ingredients and present it as "real cheese." If we can convince enough people that it's real cheese — it's frigging real cheese!

We will teach you that having a flat stomach is the most important thing in your life and you will be judged accordingly. Next year, we'll be focusing on your a$$. Don't think for a second that we are done with you.

We will make you count carbs — you are no longer just what you eat — you're a net number. We will also sell you fifty-two other diet choices since there's a 98.5% chance that you just hopelessly surrender to the total confusion and buy them all since you don't want to miss out on anything.

We pride ourselves with anorexic fashion advertising. Want to look like one of us? Skip a few meals and vomit up the dough!

We will teach you new and hip lingo — your pathetic self can become cool now — all thanks to us.

Women *always* pick their men based on the beer they drink — where have you been?

You do need V10 horsepower and four-wheel-drive in your car — you never know what disaster can happen without it. And, it's *only* $99 down! To keep your spirit up, we will only mention the remaining 379 monthly payments of $750 in illegible fine print.

If we could use "orgasmic" instead of "organic" — we would.

The bigger — the better and more important we will make you feel. It's our pledge to super-size your desperation for value and to fully support your ever-growing entitlement.

Quality = Quantity. Got it?

If we have a product that can make an erection last for over five hours — by accident or not — we want the credit, despite the potential need for medical attention (knock on wood).

We have to hire spokesmodels since you're a bunch of star-struck, pathetic followers, and we are too ugly to be shown on camera.

We make greed acceptable — it works for us, it will work for you.

We have to sell you illusions, since the real thing isn't good enough.

We hope you have enjoyed this (court-appointed and truth serum-enhanced) message.

Should you have any questions, feel free to contact us at 1-888-IN-YOUR-DREAMS or via email at directly2trash@s&m.con.

Sincerely,

$&M.CON ($ales and Marka-ching.con)
A division of HellOnEarth, Inc.

SECRET INGREDIENT

Hatred, feared by many but understood by few.

Hatred, sometimes a conviction, plan, or chosen way. A partial internal paralysis based on primitive fear or personal injustices, without a clear sense of retribution.

Hatred, the result of wounded, traumatized, and hopeless love, transitioned into a state of internal rage and immense overwhelming sadness.

Hatred, felt valid. As real and alive as any other state of mind. Its power convincing, speaking directly to our most primitive senses. Provides an outlet.

Hatred, an emotional escape that supports a fake sense of justice in a distorted personal universe. Possession of pain too vast to process, an entitlement to vent is born, producing a false sense of relief and satisfaction.

Hatred can be repaired and disposed. Sometimes. We learn to live with many things. But with Hatred, we must live to learn to love again.

SINKING INTO LOVE

A sublime palette of effervescent stimuli making ubiquitous affirmations of belonging.

THE ACC(ID)ENT

What we say matters a lot. How we say it, can matter equally much. It's easy sometimes to twist and turn something solid into something new which then takes on a very different meaning. For example: What if someone couldn't properly pronounce "peace" or "piece" and it ended up sounding like "piss" instead?

The John Lennon song would be called "Give Piss a Chance."

The environmental organization "Greenpiss" would fight liquid causes.

You could join the "Piss Corps."

"UN Piss Keepers" would restore order in the bathroom line and the entire "Piss Process."

Native Americans smoked "piss pipe."

Meditation, if done in "piss and quiet," could lead to "piss of mind."

You could order a "piss of pie" for lunch and a "piss of cake" for dessert.

Herman Wouk's classic rewritten: *War and Piss.*

The Police, sworn to "keep and uphold the piss," would arrest anyone for "disturbing the piss."

A part of the traditional wedding ceremony would be spoken as "Speak now or forever hold your piss..."

When someone dies, people would wish them to "Rest in piss..."

Would a "piss offering" between Israel and Palestine really be a good thing? Can they ever really "live in piss" with each other?

You could be married by a "justice of the piss."

And finally: You could win the "Nobel Piss Prize"!

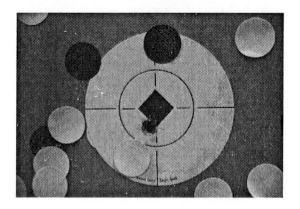

THE CIRCLE'S CENTER

The unconditional commitment and surrender to be your true self at all times without the dependency of external confirmation or approval.

THE GAME

I tell you that I'm fine when I'm not. I show interest out of politeness. I give you what you want to receive, not what I want to give. I allow you to break my sacred boundaries.

I do this to protect myself. Protect my secret self. I give you the person I want to be. I protect who I am.

You give me reasons to continue my quest. You are only interested in making your options available. You encourage behavior tailored to your taste and abilities. You have no interest to find out who I am.

My usefulness is addicting. I have purpose in my fraudulent projection. My flexibility for a greater cause is endless. I only fear no longer being needed.

What will I do when the show ends? Audition for another play? A chameleon in disguise can fool many.

The game continues without a winner.

THE GIFT

Like a circus performance, life unfolds. Trained acts, trained responses. To be noticed, more complexity is required. Only some classics remain.

A weathered clown, truth serum injected. A smile glued to a sinking ship. In desperation, more pain inflicted to attract. Always a success with a bloodthirsty crowd.

With risk higher, the acrobat triples the doubles. Can't afford fear, can't afford to lose. Must keep balance on new, thinner rope. Always younger new hope to replace you.

The rage of imprisonment, animals vent. Freedom lost, no reason to comply. Obstinate at heart, performs to kill time. Back to the cage to die some more.

The owner licks his greedy fingers. A friend with customers, a foe with staff. They are performing his name, all in forced tradition. An acrobatic show of flexibility and imprisoned hope.

Pity to the performer of daily pretend. Walking around in protective survival. Dream of the alternative, a subconscious hope and risk.

To sufficiently be yourself, a gift seldom used.

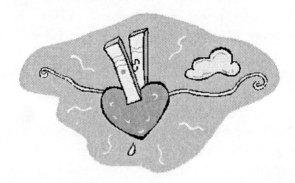

THE GREAT VOID

Filled with instinctive yearning, she reaches out.
Wishing for simple results from complex matters.
When the going gets tough, she retreats to her
guarded vault. The risk of humility interferes
with desired rewards.

Aware of personal limitations but not in charge
of their fix. Letting conditions dictate the
possibilities of what to give. Sharing what's
needed but not what really counts. A conditional
lover, in love with protection.

Guarding and preserving the sometimes unknown
self. Can't let others touch what is most frail. No
gain is worth the risk of full exposure. No pain is
ever greater than her own.

Obsessed with personal shortcomings, excuses
dominate. Some acknowledgments, the limit
of her efforts. Emotionally greedy by fear,

the heart held hostage. A beautiful flower not
allowed to bloom.

Lonely in thought and heart, a death he mourns.
Have to detach from the dream, it simply will
not be. Entering new roads unpaved, but he
keeps looking back. Wondering what was real,
hating what wasn't.

How it hurts to discover the truth, a faith lost.
A longing for more than the scope, frames now
visible. How can one be so blind through the
eyes of real love? Or is it simply a foolish belief
that it has no limits?

Inside the heart, the ghost sings alone.

THE MOTHERSHIP VS. LOCAL 101

The Case

In the early fall of 2005, an unprecedented event took place in Boston, Massachusetts. The body of a male in his mid-forties suddenly shut down and fell into a deep coma. The physical being of the male, referred to as the "MotherShip," had experienced an internal mutiny caused by most of its internal components, referred to as members of the "Local 101" union. Allegedly, the MotherShip had severely abused its relationship with Local 101 and broken most rules and regulations according to the current statute. In a desperate attempt to end the miserable working conditions for its members, Local 101 sued the MotherShip and was granted a Temporary Shutdown Order so proper proceedings could be held without external interference.

The legal entity Universal Heritage of Humans (UH-OH) reacted quickly. Due to time constraints, it was decided that mediation proceedings would start immediately with all parties present in the MotherShip Boardroom, located inside the individual. An UH-OH legal team was sent to handle the proceedings.

Honorable Judge Cerebellum was chosen to preside. The judge had impressive experience and was calm, very detail-oriented, and aware of everything in motion and progress.

Arthur Wrath was selected to represent Local 101. Wrath had a long successful career prosecuting petty offenses related to the Statute of Public Opinion.

Representing the MotherShip was attorney Polly Ester-Rash. She was mostly famous for defending the Ben Dover Act of 1979 — the biggest ongoing labor law dispute ever — producing a bill of rights for corporate players.

The first mediation attempt failed miserably. Both parties were in a state of shock which resulted in even more chaos. There was so much confusion that Judge Cerebellum ordered a recess until the following day so the parties could get their act together without jeopardizing critical life-support functions of the MotherShip.

The MotherShip boardroom was located on the Visual Cortex of the now-comatose individual. It was a fairly large room with a conference table situated in the middle and sunken ceiling lights. There were no windows, but the room had two large screens used for displaying the view from each eye via optic nerve cable-feed. Since the individual was currently in a coma, the screens were black. Along the sides of the room were dozens of smaller monitors, each providing operative stats for various organs and body functions.

There was a dreadful silence in the MotherShip boardroom that August morning, right before the second proceeding took place. The room was crowded and the air was thin. Opposing sides were seated on each side of the table — staring into the air under the slightly dimmed lights. Suddenly, Judge Cerebellum entered the room from his makeshift chambers located in an adjacent office. He walked briskly over to the large chair at the end of table.

"Please remain seated," he said with a brief hand gesture.

"Ok, since time is of the essence, let's get started. Are all parties present?"

"Arthur Wrath representing Local 101, Your Honor."

"Your Honor, Polly Ester-Rash representing the MotherShip."

"Good," said the judge, "I assume you have summoned all your witnesses and that they are all present?"

"Yes, Your Honor," said Arthur Wrath and Polly Ester-Rash at the same time.

"Very well then," said Judge Cerebellum, "Before we proceed with opening statements, I must set a few ground rules based on what happened yesterday. First, I herby pronounce all of you under oath. Second, I will allow several witnesses to be questioned at the same time by both sides in the interest of continuity. This may seem a bit unorthodox but based on the apparent codependency that exists, we must do what we can to allow the truth, and nothing but the whole truth, to come out. Mr. Wrath, you may proceed."

Arthur Wrath stood up and walked to the back of his chair.

"Thank you, Your Honor," said Wrath. "We will demonstrate that the MotherShip has failed to provide a safe and dignifying work environment for all of the Local 101 members, hence claiming they have broken their current contract. We will show that even after repeated attempts by Local

101 to contact the MotherShip management to warn them about the atrocities, they ignored all warnings and expected work to continue as usual. Thank you."

"Your turn," said Judge Cerebellum, looking at Polly Ester-Rash.

"Thank you, Your Honor. Contrary to the statement you just heard, we will show that the MotherShip is not at fault for any of the current conditions since it's entirely caused by the disarray within Local 101 itself. That's it. Thank you."

"Thank you," said Judge Cerebellum. "Local 101 may call its first witness."

"Thank you, Your Honor. We call Logic to the stand."

Logic looked around the room.
"I do not compute," said Logic. "I don't see a stand."
"Just a protocol formality," said Judge Cerebellum. "Please remain seated and proceed."
Wrath turned towards Logic.
"So, in your opinion as acting manager of daily operations, what is really going on here?"
"It is difficult to compile a patentable answer to that question, but I can compute a high

probability assessment. Speaking for my section only, I have the ability to reason, to execute, to learn, etc., but my features have not been used much. I'm under-utilized and most of the time I have to compete with Habit, who has no reasoning powers at all. This goes against the terms of my contract and it has created chaos in areas where I'm supposed to participate. Habit cannot do my job under any circumstances — he's just a predictable copycat. There are also cooperation issues between other members that have prevented my active participation in the daily operations of the MotherShip. On top of that, some of the equipment is defective, need upgrades or repairs. We can't do our jobs during these circumstances."

"So how do you feel about that?" said Polly Ester-Rash.

"I do not compute," said Logic, "ask Emotions."

Wrath looked at Emotions.

"So what does Emotions have to add to the previous statement?"

Emotion looked as if it was about to cry.

"Oh, I don't know...it's just SOOO SAD. I mean, I've tried to like talk to everyone and 'walk in their shoes,' create bonds, take interest, and get involved as much as possible but there are just sooooooooooo many problems and it makes me feel like, uh, soooooooooo heavy! I just want to run and hide, which I do a lot these days,

actually. Anyways, um, the current operations of the MotherShip have caused me like soooooooo much distress, confusion and trauma that I had to like protect myself in any way possible."
"You had no building permit for putting up walls," interrupted Logic.
"Oh, I know, I knooooooooow, but I *had to* protect myself, see — I'm fragile and didn't know what to do many times. I'm soooooo lonely, you know! Nobody talks to me anymore! See, I need feedback from everyone in order to do my work! I need communication!"

Polly Ester-Rash turned to Logic.
"So, Logic, since you and Emotions clearly are the 'foremen' of your organization, what have you done to accomplish a more stable environment for your workers?"
"We agreed to try to meet halfway, Emotions and I," said Logic, "but many normal function calls get rerouted to other areas for reasons unknown to me."
"Please give me an example of those other areas," said Polly Ester-Rash.
"Well, Private Richard is one with sometimes disastrous results. His interference makes it very difficult to come to an agreement on things."
"Who is Private Richard?" said Judge Cerebellum.
"Oh, I'm sorry, it's the 'Private Parts.' We call him Private Richard per his own request," said Emotions.

"Yeah, but others *still* call me lots of other things," said Private Richard, "I get 'Dickie,' 'Tiny Tim,' 'Salami Boy,' and 'Dumb-Stick' most of the time. This verbal abuse has to end!"

"I've seen you create fake itches just to get attention," said Logic.

"Oh, shut up, Robot Boy! What the hell do you know about it? You haven't seen what I have seen or been where I've been!"

"So you blame your working conditions for your actions?" interrupted Wrath.

"Objection, Your Honor," said Polly Ester-Rash, "Counselor is leading the witness."

"Overruled," said Judge Cerebellum, "I want to hear this. The witness may proceed."

"Your Honor, I have had a very stressful life from years of abuse, overuse and constantly being forced to go on missions in dark, slippery places. Sometimes even without protective gear! I mean HELLO — how fun is it to come out with more than you came in with? And to add to the fun, a small army of merchant antibodies is many times required to remove the new 'muck' clinging on to my equipment! Usually, once the troops have arrived, those fights can last for seven to ten days! I am pretty much disabled during these battles and nobody warned me either! Just out of the blue — hello itch, rash, discharge! Merry friggin' Christmas! I mean, I have a reputation to protect too! What will my parents think if they find out? Huh?"

"So, what about you, Liver? Have anything to add?" said Polly Ester-Rash.
"I see purple bunnies...hi hi hi...lotsa little fuzzy purple bunnies...come here, bunny...come here..."
"Your Honor, Defense moves to have Liver disqualified as a reliable witness. It is too damaged to testify."

Judge Cerebellum took a long sad look at Liver. "As much as it saddens me, I'm inclined to agree. Motion granted. Move along."

After a pause with a frozen, horrified look on his face, Wrath took a deep breath.

"Stomach, your complaint is listed as 'excessive pollution.' Can you please elaborate?"
"Hot dogs, pizza, hot dogs, pizza and more friggin' hot dogs! That's the bulk of what was coming in. Do you know what's in those things? Well, I do and it ain't pretty trying to distribute the crap! Then, add daily gallons of soda and beer, greasy potatoes, and chips and salsa to the equation and you have one acidic cesspool to manage. Forget the weekends, or 'rainy season' as we call it down here — all you see is beer, more beer, friggin' peanuts and pizza! Do you know how long it takes me to break down peanuts? Forty-eight friggin' hours!
"So how were you trying to warn the MotherShip of what was going on?" asked Polly Ester-Rash.

"Ha! Funny you should mention it! I radioed upstairs telling them to send both Hunger and Craving on an indefinite leave and to block off the intake valve by any means possible. Then, I started turning on more acid pumps in order to keep up with the huge quantities consumed by the MotherShip. I admit I got so pissed off sometimes that just threw everything that came in unprocessed directly into trash pipeline and back-flushed some of the acid so he would get a taste of what we were dealing with down here. What does the idiot do then? He starts chewing gum! Who the hell approved that?!"

"There's no record of gum approval in my database," said Logic.

"I think it was Habit but he probably didn't mean it," said Emotions. "I mean, he really doesn't know 'why' he does anything anyway."

"Ah, that just great — protect the offender," yelled Stomach.

"Oh, I'm soooo not protecting him — just trying to understand why he does what he does based on his limitations, you know," said Emotions.

"Go and hug an artery, you hippie!" yelled Private Richard.

"Hey, watch it, Needle Boy! I can disable your mechanics, remember, and what are you going to do then, with a defective compass?" screamed Emotions.

"Order in the court," yelled Judge
Cerebellum, "I will not tolerate these kinds of
outbursts! Understood? Who's next in line?"

Polly Ester-Rash briefly glanced at a piece of
paper.
"Plumbing, you have been described as an
'oddball' by your co-workers. Why is that?"
"I don't know," said Plumbing. "Maybe they lack
a certain sense of humor."
"And what sense of humor would that be?" said
Polly Ester-Rash.
"Having my job, one needs to do all things
possible to cope and laugh as much as possible.
For example, I created an alarm system that uses
musical alerts. Every time a kidney stone is on
the move, I play Rolling Stones songs. When the
host needs to pass gas, I play Bach's 'Air.' I'm
working on a complete playlist, actually."
"Ok, that's nice," said Polly Ester-Rash. "But
it also says here that you are a writer. Please
explain."
"I write to amuse myself — it's that simple."
"Clearly, but some of your co-workers were
pretty offended by some of your writings. In
particular, the weekly *Internal Examiner*. What's
that all about?"
"It's a humorous gossip column I produce. It's
just for laughs."
"That might be the intent but who's
laughing other than you? Allow me to read
some headlines: 'Water Gate — the Bladder

Scandals,' 'Emotional Defenses Sold at Wall
Mart,' 'Heart Skips a Beat and Joins Rappers
Run EKG,' 'Proof: Rectum Wrote *Winnie the
Pooh*!' 'Shocker: All Uptight A-holes Arrived
to America on Ship Called *The Constipation*,'
'Is Esophagus Deep Throat?' 'Hair Splits with
Scalp — Curley Falls off Deep End — Goes on
Rogaine Binge — We Have the Before and After
Pictures!'"

Polly Ester-Rash looked at Plumbing.

"Yeah, what's your point?" said Plumbing.
"Don't you think that some of this can be
considered offensive?"
"It's not intended to be."
"Someone needs their screws tightened," said
Logic.
"Oh, come on, man! Lighten up! Since when is
everything so bloody serious? Let's face it, I have
a shitty job and I need to amuse myself in order
to cope. It's just creativity! If you want the real
juicy stuff, I'm not it. Ask DNA."
"Ask DNA about what?" said Polly Ester-Rash.
"I'm not giving you the poop on that one since
you already possess the information," said
Plumbing.

Judge Cerebellum looked in his papers.
"I don't see any records of DNA in the submitted
paperwork. Why is that?"

"Your Honor," said Polly Ester-Rash, "we have had some 'behavioral issues' with DNA. It was discovered that DNA had hacked into every database in the MotherShip and planted viruses and spyware. It took us over six months to recover from these attacks."
"So you *do* have problems with your own people but are trying to cover it up, eh?" said Arthur Wrath with a grin.
"Your Honor, we felt that our own internal investigation as well as the constructive counteractions that followed was nobody's business but our own."
"Whatever happened to professional courtesy?" snapped Arthur Wrath.
"I tend to agree," said Judge Cerebellum, "You should have notified the management of Local 101 and alerted them of the potential risk. You have an obligation of full disclosure to the tenant under the current stature that you cannot ignore."
"Point taken, Your Honor," said Polly Ester-Rash. "My apologies. It won't happen again."

Arthur Wrath looked around the room.
"Skin, what's on your list?"
"The exterior maintenance is a friggin' nightmare! How can anyone allow such a dirtbag to roam free? There is a constant pimple war going on in the oversized, greasy, toxic pores! Man, they are so huge you can park a friggin' bus in there! Also, what's up with those nuclear

armpits, people? I know this guy went through
basic training and is aware of soap and water,
so why doesn't he use it? By the way, where's
my hazardous pay for the bomb-making material
called feet! We are aging a lot faster due to this,
people — we look old! We look OLD!!!"

"Conscience, what's your take on the situation?"
said Arthur Wrath.
"Uhm...I would like to evoke my Fifth
Amendment right not to incriminate myself."
"You can't, since this court is not abiding by
traditional amendment rights," said judge
Cerebellum. "You are to tell the truth — and the
whole truth. Please proceed."
"Well then...I know of a lot of 'stuff' that doesn't
get out in the open since it has been labeled
classified by the MotherShip. You're telling me
it's ok to ignore that now?"
"Yes," said the judge.
"Phew...that's a first. Gee, I don't know where
to begin. I know this guy has a lot of regrets.
The list is so long today since things have gotten
out of hand over the years. Deep down, he
'wants to' do things differently but he can't
today — it's all too much — too big. Everything
has 'dominoed' beyond recognition and it's very
difficult to find the original source for things.
What's really real? I don't..."

"I'll tell you what's real," interrupted Intuition.
"I've been violated! I've been a prisoner for

soooooooo long, under such awful conditions that in comparison would be similar to those experienced by Nelson Mandela! What's the point with suppressing me, huh? When am I going to be released??? I want justice!"

"Order!" said Judge Cerebellum firmly. "Points duly noted but please wait for your turn. Now, please proceed and let's be civilized."

Polly Ester-Rash turned to Intellect.
"Intellect, your resume is quite impressive. A good education, strong parental relationship and guidance, processed and digested a lot of culture and arts. I would say you have been very well taken care of. Wouldn't you agree?"
"Well...," said Intellect, pausing briefly, "It started out ok but things got progressively worse."
"Please be specific," said Polly Ester-Rash.
"I was well taken care of and stimulated for a long time. But for the last fifteen years or so, it's been going downhill. I was given less and less of my needed stimuli in order to function and grow and I have no idea what caused the flow to stop. Logic, Emotions, and I used to sit down and chat. We created many connections and pathways in those days which really produced a balanced working environment for everyone. Even the MotherShip would utilize its Power Savings Mode, or "Sleep" as they call it, better in those days so the equipment could get a brake. Nowadays, it's

like an everlasting Formula One race where you
have 6.9 seconds to take a piss or eat, otherwise
you'll fall behind in the race. What race is this
guy running anyway? What's there to win? I don't
get it."

"So what kind of stimuli are you getting these
days?" asked Arthur Wrath.

"Ah, that would be none. I am mostly exposed
to meaningless sports stats, cartoons, and news
digests as far as reading is concerned. On top of
that, endless hours of watching sports, B-movies,
and reality TV. What am I supposed to do with
that? I feel like I'm swimming 400 daily laps
at the shallow end of the pool, people. I feel
transparent!"

"I've always been able to see right through you,"
said Private Richard.

"Ah, the voice of the Primitive Private," said
Intellect.

"You are such a snob and you're just jealous that
I get utilized more than you. Sure, I don't have
your 'education' but man, do I have more hours
logged! How do you feel about that, Buffy?"
yelled Private Richard.

"Hey Squirt Gun," said Intellect, "I will not argue
meaningless instinctual behavior with you since
you can't comprehend anything else."

"Enough!" yelled Judge Cerebellum. "In my
chambers — now!"

Judge Cerebellum, Arthur Wrath, and Polly
Ester-Rash sat down inside the judge's
chambers.

"So, what's going on here?" said the judge with
a concerned look.

"Your Honor, if I may?" said Arthur Wrath.

"Please," said the judge.

"Your Honor, I apologize for the disarray, but this
is a very serious situation. Everyone is on edge
due to the circumstances but we strongly feel
that this very unfortunate situation is caused by
a lack of leadership from the MotherShip. Our
members are acting 100% from the directives
given in the provided environment. I don't see
how we carry any of the blame here."

"Your Honor," said Polly Ester-Rash, "of course,
we are sorry about the circumstances as well but
we have provided as much leadership to Local
101 as this individual has allowed us to."

"Please explain," said the judge.

"First of all, let's recognize the total absence
of a manual or user's guide. There isn't one
for human beings — there has never been one
either. We get all of our information from
external, scattered sources that we later
introduce to the individual for processing in Mr.
Wrath's department. We get bombarded with
information on a daily basis. We have no way
of telling, ahead of time, if the information
is or is not applicable to the individual. Also,
the information can be very conflicting. One
day, something is reported good, and the next,

the same thing can cause problems. At best, it's an overload of conflicts! Believe me, the MotherShip is doing its very best to supply only reliable, applicable information and solutions for the individual but we are fighting an uphill battle. For example, there are several sources of advice or information for individuals. You have medical information, religious advice, nutritional information, society, fashion, etc., all delivered to us but we can not be held responsible if the individual doesn't apply what he or she needs. That's where Mr. Wrath's department comes in and that is why we feel that we are entirely without blame in this matter."

"Hmm, interesting points," said the judge. "Anything to add, Mr. Wrath?"

"Your Honor, while some of the points from my esteemed colleague are valid, I'm afraid we simply see things from different perspectives. We have an amazing fleet of very talented workers here. When is it ever ok to deliver conflicting information or not to respond to warning signals given by our staff? And, based on that, expect things to work? Are we supposed to rely on luck, fiction, or facts? Last time I checked, we were not in the gaming business. While I sympathize with the difficult task of assessing information validity and applicability, we feel that it is a requirement as a part of the existing lease agreement. Their responsibility doesn't end with gathering and delivering info — they have to verify it as well as maintain facilities and equipment despite sometimes less desirable conditions. Garbage in, garbage out — it's that simple and not such a big surprise."

"Good points, Mr. Wrath," said the judge. "Purgamentum init — exit purgamentum. But, I'm afraid there's more to this case than what either of you have brought up so far."

Arthur Wrath and Polly Ester-Rash sat quietly. Neither of them felt they could sensibly contribute to what the judge had just said. They had too many vested interests and didn't want to expose any potential weaknesses.

"Ok," said Judge Cerebellum after a brief silence. "I need to evaluate the situation in private. You will have my ruling once I'm done. Due to the complex nature of this case and its circumstances, it might take awhile."
"Thank you, Your Honor," said Arthur Wrath and Polly Ester-Rash, and they left the judge's chambers.

The judge sat quietly in his chair. This was a tough one, indeed. He thought about other cases he had been involved in. "What has happened to humans?" he thought. "Things used to be more clear and simple and not so immensely complex as in this case. No unity and total detachment. Why?"

He leaned back and closed his eyes. It would be a couple of days before he would be ready — he already knew that. "Where would this end?" he thought. "How did we end up here? This case clearly required him to closely examine things and possibly go places he wasn't entirely comfortable with. It had to be done, however.

The Ruling

Forty-eight hours after the last failed mediation attempt, the parties were told to gather in the MotherShip boardroom. Judge Cerebellum entered the room and sat down. He looked long and hard at all the faces in the room. Nobody made a sound.

After looking down for a moment, the judge started speaking.
"How does one define ultimate ownership and responsibility in this case? Is it even possible? Also, based on testimony so far, what is actual habit vs. natural defense vs. rebellion? Nobody is intentionally destructive, yet damage is still done. Quite a dilemma.

"I've spent time over the last two days watching video archives of our subject individual.
It proved to be very helpful. Since nobody bothered to present me with a more complete

picture of him, due to present vested interests, allow me to do it for you.

"Our subject's name is Bill and is in his mid-forties. Single, never married, steady job as a salesman, no pets, no plants — just Bill and his buddies. He's about 6'4". Bill appears to have ignored a lot of things — in particular things related to himself. His general health has become an issue over the last couple of years. His doctor warned him about the risks he was facing by not doing something constructive about it. But, Bill showed little effort in creating any change. His parents were really concerned about their son, too, and tried helping him as much as they could. However, nothing appears to have had an effect on the bottom line. Why?

"Bill clearly felt paralyzed facing the task of change, so he escaped, both mentally and physically. He enjoyed many things, primarily those in excess. He loved good food and plenty of it. When he drank, he drank a lot. When he went shopping, he overspent. There were many handy Band-Aids to cover up or remedy the real issues. Going to extremes made him temporarily forget his problems and disappear into a fantasy world much more manageable than his painful, boring reality. Many times, the extreme action could mean doing absolutely nothing.

"His job as a salesman was based on the principle of acting a part. Bill could become whoever he wanted to be and be rewarded financially for it. To Bill, this was really an amazing blessing and he loved doing it. After many years of practice, the acting and pretending became the norm throughout his life. The eternal escape appeared to be here to stay and it would take a miracle for things to change. Bill had lost touch with himself and the reality in front of him. The rest, you already know.

"So, one may ask, why this guy? Why not Joe or Jane Schmo down the street? The more I look at this case, the more convinced I get that it's a somewhat random event. However, it's only random because it actually came this far. I'm sure there are millions, possibly billions, of people in very similar situations but they don't suffer a breakdown or internal mutiny. What is the difference between these people and our subject? What sets them apart?

"The answer in our case is lack of global adaptation inside the individual. Reality and the people in it have changed and one has to adapt. This is not an option — it's a must. The policies and procedures of both parties present today are very outdated and obsolete in many aspects. Your old ways are too slow. Signals sent are not detected anymore since today's pace is much faster or has a different frequency. You have continued to base all operations and procedures on how things were ten to fifteen years ago. You all have lost track of the internal and external development status and its very important relationship to the individual. Through the years, you have proceeded in your usual fashion without checking if the same conditions apply. You all have lost touch and the very unfortunate end-result is the breakdown of your host. He is completely lost, and very much thanks to you.

"Therefore, it is my ruling that everyone is equally at fault in this case. I hold every single one of you responsible for the current conditions. However, for the record, I would like to point out that nobody did anything intentionally for this operation to fail. It's a lack of growth, development and adaptation on your part that is missing. You are so used to giving all your focus to the individual's development and operations that you 'forgot' to update or adapt yourself in the process. To keep an amazing vessel like a human being running and progressing is a very daunting task that requires absolute internal synchronicity. We all make mistakes at times or could do things better — that's not the issue here. It is your duty and obligation, not society, the government or even this court, to uphold a great standard and be sensitive and alert to needed changes and modifications to current procedures.

Everything is always in constant transition and you must learn to adapt. It's a very reasonable expectation.

"Furthermore, I hereby dissolve both management teams effective immediately since they have proven ineffective and harmful to the host. You are never to be separated by jurisdiction, or other, from this moment on. You are to work and co-exist under one roof, one management. To be one, that is the purpose. You will sit down together and you will figure this out. Considered it ordered.

"In closing, I find the lack of an official operations guide or manual for human beings ludicrous. Sure, there are many different cultures, different kinds of people with equally many personalities, traditions, and heritages. However, they all have so much in common. I find it unacceptable to have inaccurate and unreliable information available in regards to things that can threaten the existence or well-being of humans, animals or plant life, despite complexities at hand. Furthermore, I find it equally unacceptable allowing the media to exploit these speculations with what appears to be infinite variables for unrelated purposes and personal gain. What is it going to take to permanently filter out what doesn't work and shield society's non-scientific members from conflicting information and placebo-like products? At the same time, let's acknowledge and applaud all the working discoveries that have been produced to aid.

"I want this case to represent a big section of the ink used on the formal request for a high-level investigation into these issues I intend to file with the highest court. There is too much pain, suffering, and conflict in the world as it is. Every living being should receive the ability or chance to experience a happy and balanced existence. Each life form is very precious and deserves more value and respect than what it is currently receiving. Once this has been accomplished, a much less destructive society will exist where needed lessons can be learned constructively, and hopefully with less demolition.

"This court is adjourned."

Epilogue

Nobody has contested the ruling to date.

Subject Bill did wake up. He has no clue as to what happened, but is doing well.

Judge Cerebellum was commended and promoted for his work in this case. He now enjoys his new position as executive producer for Stephen Hawking's daily brain broadcasts for aliens on undetectable frequencies.

Arthur Wrath left the court system and went back to his hobby of selling emotional real estate and Caribbean guilt trips.

Polly Ester-Rash met her future husband, Urethane, and changed jobs a few years later to manage their joint "Polly & Urethane Packing Materials" business. She remains the primary shareholder in Gold Bond Medicated.

Logic recompiled itself and is said to perform better after rebooting.

Emotions had a fling with Intuition upon its release from prison. They were last seen on a beach, smoking clove cigarettes in the nude.

Liver checked into the Betty Ford Clinic under the assumed name Purple B. Unnies. It is expected to recover and resume its duties as Director of the Internal X-Files Foundation.

Stomach eventually got the license to manufacture "Belly Beans" candy. Sales have been a bit low due to competitor Cornea's Eye Candy.

Plumbing perused its dream of cutting a flatulence version of Queen's "Bohemian

Rhapsody." It was released, picked up and later distributed by Wosh-Bang! Records. A homemade screenplay for *Gone with the Wind — The Cyclone Aftermath* is also said to be in the works.

DNA assumed the alias "AND" in order to prove its reformed hacker status. It now designs scientific puzzles at Genome Toys, Inc.

Skin took a much-needed vacation to Hawaii and is rumored to have had binged Hawaiian Tropic for two weeks straight. To remedy the damages done, it checked itself into Botox upon returning.

Conscience was further interrogated regarding its role preceding the case. It had a nervous breakdown after blowing all the fuses in the lie detector and was later replaced with a fresh copy.

Intellect challenged itself to invent a game based on infinite chess, dimensions from Fermat's Theorem and known formulas of cold fusion. It hasn't been seen or heard from since but is expected to return.

Private Richard joined the Church of Power Tools and legally changed its name to Stanley Decker. It still creates fake itches for attention, but with less frequency... ☺

THE NEW RESIDENT

My dad has moved into a new place. The estate is located on high ground with plenty of open space. He lives on the top floor and the view is spectacular. The place is fully customized and automated in every possible aspect to suit him. No cleaning. No grocery shopping. No cooking. No repairs or upkeep needed. Total comfort. There are many places to eat, too. Visit any restaurant or eat at home. All-inclusive.

There are plenty of things to do. He has lots of friends and relatives in the neighborhood to hang out with when he feels like it. There are a variety of concerts everywhere — for each and every taste. Plenty of nice places to go for a walk or jog. The area is really safe and clean, too. The weather and climate are simply perfect.

Knowing my dad, he will get a bit bored at times with the level of comfort. Not that he enjoys handiwork or cooking, but sometimes he likes throwing a bag of frozen Swedish meatballs in a frying pan and cooking some pasta himself. Needless to say, the dishes would be done immediately after the meal. Later, there better be good ice cream and snacks around.

I'm not sure what wine and cheese assortments are available. After all, he is a connoisseur and may need to have a few "words" with the management if something isn't to his liking or is missing. Hopefully, the crossword puzzles are intellectually challenging too. A well-assorted bookstore is a must.

But, I think they realize they are lucky to have him there and will do whatever they can to attend to his needs and desires.

I really miss having him around. My dad left Population, Earth and moved to the Heavenly Pastures Estate on May 15, 2005.

THE TRAIN RIDE — A MOTHER'S TALE

I decided to include the following story, told by my mother in her own words at numerous dinner tables over the years. It's a token of the respect and admiration I have for parents who are there for their kids as well as their perseverance based on what their children sometimes put them through. My hat goes off to you... ☺

~~~~~~~~~~~~~~~~~~~~

Our eight-year-old son, Jakob, and I had taken the overnight train from Stockholm to Gothenburg. This was the first stop on our way to a much-needed summer vacation on the west coast of Sweden. We would get picked up by my husband and younger son at the train station in Båstad, our final destination. After a bad night's sleep, I was really looking forward to a lovely breakfast buffet at Gothenburg's Central Station — one I knew about from previous travels. After breakfast, we would continue with a day-train that would take approximately two hours to our final destination.

I had prepared Jakob for what to expect. But, once we arrived at the restaurant, it was closed! Everything is always open the rest of the year, but no service during summer vacation months — typical! There was nothing available to eat within a mile's radius of the station and our train was leaving in an hour.

Our oldest son is not the most cheerful person in the morning, and I could sense a crisis was near. Our rescue was a kiosk at the station. They had all kinds of candy but no fruit. A banana would have saved the situation, for sure. The not-so-cheerful-in-the-morning son got in a really good mood once he received a bag of gummy bears at that hour, and suddenly all risks of collision were gone. With his bag of candy and a copy of the latest *Superman,* we boarded the train that would take us along the coast to Båstad.

Finally, the train got going and we were on our way! Jakob read his *Superman* magazine and diligently ate from his bag of candy. I found yesterday's paper in my bag and was trying to read it. I was really hungry so it was difficult to concentrate.

Suddenly, Jakob put down his magazine in his lap, glanced out the window for a brief moment, then looked right at me and said with a strong voice:

"You've done it, haven't you?"
He stared at me with great anticipation.

"Done what, Jakob?" I said.
"You know...*it*..."

I noted a small "movement" in our fellow passengers. Being his mother, I suspected what he was referring to and I felt I owed him an honest answer.

"Yes, Jakob," I replied as calmly and quietly as possible.
"Twice, huh?" (We have two children.)

What do you answer your child on a question like this? Do you agree and potentially give him the wrong impression for life? I bravely decided to be as honest as possible.

"I think it has happened more than twice."
"What? Several times? WHEN?"

"Jakob! I can't tell you when. It's just
something that happens now and then."

He seemed really upset. I also noticed a growing
interest in this interrogation from our fellow
passengers.

"Was it the night before we left?" he continued.
"I can't tell you when it was!"
"Was it the other night when I came home
after..."
"Jakob! It wasn't then, and I can't remember
when it was last!"

There were a few moments of dead silence.
Then, with a very loud and clear voice, he said:
"No, Birgitta, *that* I didn't believe about you!
Really not! WHEN WAS THE LAST TIME?"

Everything suddenly became deadly silent.
I felt like my situation was being judged by
the spectators. When was it last? Would I
tell? Behind my paper of yesterday's news,
I was trying to keep my calm, very irritated
by everyone who was trying to find out more
about my private life. I did not appreciate the
entertainment that Jakob and I had contributed
our fellow passengers with this Sunday morning.
Why wasn't the father here to solve the situation
in a rational way?

Jakob sat down and pondered his newfound view about his mom. Whatever he thought, he did in silence. It appeared to be all over, then suddenly:

"But, seriously, Birgitta, is it really true? I would never had thought that about you! Have there been other men, too?"

I didn't answer the last, and very dangerous, question in a pedagogical way. I whispered to Jakob that he and I would speak about this later — *in private*. And like magic, we had reached our final destination! Jakob and I were the only two passengers who departed the train. As we exited, everyone was giving us long, sad looks.

Several days after this trip, Jakob returned to the subject matter and the fact that he was very "disappointed" in me. That I had done "it" more than twice, that is. But he never raised the question regarding other men again and for that, I am grateful.

Moral of the story: Don't give kids candy for breakfast — you *never* know what may happen!

Jakob Wahlberg

WHAT I WISH FOR YOU

May you always know you have a place.
May you never feel alone.
May you always have forgiveness.

May you never lose hope.
May you always be loved for who you are.
May you never lose your identity.

May you always feel special.
May you never feel left outside.
May you always embrace the present.

May you never live in the past.
May you always look forward.
May you never ever forget your way back.

May you always know I love you.
May you never doubt your heart.
May you always want to share yourself.

May you always know I would do anything.
May you never live behind walls.
May you always feel worthy.

May you always know you are the inspiration
behind these words.

Jakob Wahlberg

WHAT WAS I THINKING?

What was I thinking? Going to the furthest edge on the limb?

What was I thinking? Believing it was possible?

What was I thinking? Sacrificing against better judgment?

What was I thinking? Allowing myself to get hurt?

What was I thinking? Opening up my doors?

What was I thinking? Letting down my walls?

What was I thinking? Having faith in good intentions?

What was I thinking? That I would receive the same in return?

I wasn't thinking.

I was feeling.

WHEN IN DOUBT

"Welcome to Customer Service. How may I assist you today?"

"Yes, hi, I'd like to make an exchange."

"Ok. Which product is this in regard to?"

"Life."

"Ok. When was the product purchased?"

"Uh, you mean when was I born?"

"Well, no — that's when the product was activated."

"I don't understand."

"I need the approximate date of creation."

"How am I supposed to know that?"

"Well, try to remember if you were born early or late and then count backwards nine months from there."

"Oh, ok...hang on...about early September 1963."

"Ok, thank you. Please hold while I access our warranty records for that period... Sir, thank you for holding. Do you have your serial number handy so I can verify your subscription to technical support?"

"What serial number? Where is it located?"

"Based on the time of activation, you may have been registered using your social security number. May I have it so I can check, please?

"Ok, it's 0987-65-4321."

"Thank you. Now, what seems to be the problem with Life?"

"Well, it doesn't work."

"What do you mean, sir? Can you be more specific?"

"It doesn't perform according specifications. It says in your documentation that if I do *ABC* right, I should get *123*, but it doesn't work."

"Ok. I'm sorry to hear that Life isn't working for you. Do you mind if I ask you some more specific questions so we can troubleshoot Life further?"

"No, go ahead. I really want Life to work. I need it to work since I'm dependent on it for my livelihood."

"Ok, good. When did you first start noticing that something was wrong with Life?"

"Well, I guess the first sign was probably as a child — I got sick a lot. I mean, a lot more than everyone else."

"Did you have proper virus definitions installed?"

"Yes, I got the usual shots just like everybody else but it didn't help. My entire system just shut down at times without warning."

"Anything in the logs?"

"Not really, the medical records were not always available or even readable many times — couldn't understand half of what was in there — so cryptic and complex. The doctors were not able to diagnose why it happened the way it did."

"I'm sorry to hear that. What were other symptoms?"

"Well, later in my teens and through college, I noticed a decrease in overall performance. Everything became really sluggish and it would take forever to complete a simple task. I figured some of the symptoms could be contributed to the expanded memory and new 'storage space' for all the things I had learned. Just to be sure, I went in to have various scans and diagnostics done but they all came out clean."

"Ok. What symptoms happened after college?"

"In order to start paying off my loans and other debt, I took a job at a company. The job itself wasn't that great but I did my best to cope since I really needed the money. Also, I met a girl who I really fell in love with."

"Sounds wonderful! What was wrong with that?"

"Well, regarding the job — after a few years, the company merged with another and there were massive layoffs. Despite performing very well and following the appropriate networking protocols, I had to take a huge pay cut or get the pink slip. I just felt it was so unfair since I hadn't done anything wrong. I had to put Life in Chapter 11 for a good while since I couldn't pay all the bills. This greatly affected the relationship with my girlfriend, too."

"I'm sorry to hear that. In what way?"

"She claimed I 'stopped responding' and was too concerned with After Life."

"Did you check your Privacy and Security settings?"

"Yes, everything was at default. I felt so bad since she even made cookies for me to cheer me up! I was so scared of losing her that I froze a lot — nothing would move. She finally got tired of pushing my refresh buttons and the fact that I was out of cache so she became '404' — Cannot Be Found."

"At the time, had you added any new programs, routines or new hardware of any kind?"

"Well, I had gotten a car, a gym membership, I was on a pretty strict diet that blocked cookies and I started going to school at night for Life lessons. Based on my research, neither conflicted with the other and if anything — I should have felt better! But Life just wouldn't cooperate. Everything became a struggle and I ended up with no resources left. I was looking for Life Support for a while but couldn't afford a dialup connection or phone."

"Did you ever do a memory dump and debug?"

"Yes, I saw a therapist for a while, but he just confused the bits a lot."

"That's too bad. So, what happened next and where are you today?"

"Basically, I stayed at the company for a while but got laid off or 'ejected' two years later. They had discovered some security issues in my department where misleading information would pop up here and there and couldn't be removed. Instead of taking any chances, they reformatted the company structure and shut our partition down completely."

"Hmm...sounds like spyware."

"Could have been. Anyway, since then, I've been barely surviving doing temporary Internet filing to make ends meet. I'm in my early forties and I have little or nothing to show for it except struggles and Life experiences. Everything is slowing down even more the older I get. I just feel that Life is not what it claims to be and that mine might be defective or something. I see other people having a great Life and I'm thinking why couldn't my Life be like theirs?"

"Sir, just out of curiosity, when is the last time you rebooted?"

"What do you mean by rebooted?"

"Restarted yourself to allow all new internal settings and resources to refresh themselves."

"Uh, I have never rebooted."

"You have never rebooted? Well, that's the source of your problem right there. No wonder things aren't working! You've been growing,

adding data and experiences, updates, patches
and done a huge amount of maintenance but
none of these changes will actually take in effect
until you reboot."

"Oh, really? Geez, I didn't know that!"

"By default, you should have received indications
to do this after many of the applied changes
or upgrades. Do you recall ever receiving any
indications to do this?"

"Well, come to think of it, I guess I did but I sort
of ignored them thinking it would work anyway.
Gosh, I feel so stupid!"

"No need to feel that way, sir. Sometimes the
most simple fix is the most invisible option of
them all."

"So all I have to do is say 'yes' to accept all
settings and make a fresh start?"

"Yes, that's correct. That is a reboot.

"Hmm...so, here are some questions: What
actually happens when you reboot? Will I feel
any different afterwards? It doesn't remove
anything important just because it's old, right?"

"When you reboot, all internal information will
be refreshed and stored in its proper place.
Processing things should be much smoother since
all temporary data that doesn't apply any longer
will be gone or archived. You will feel refreshed
and at peace with many things since you now
will have a sensible and applicable perspective.
Rebooting doesn't make you forget anything
— simply manage everything better."

"Ah, that's just amazing! I wish I had known this a long time ago. Thank you very much for your help! You're a Life saver!"

"You're very welcome, sir. Thank you for calling and have a nice Life."

WISDOM

The zenith of an experienced heart, mind, and soul.

ABOUT THE AUTHOR

Swedish native Jakob Wahlberg comes from
a creative background of acting, music, and
writing.

He had his first acting role at the age of four
in Ibsen's *A Doll's House* and continued to
participate in various Swedish television drama
projects for many years, along with being a co-
host for a children's show.

He has done songwriting and music studio work
for bands, artists, and TV.

Over the years, he has done voiceover work for
Swedish Disney films and *Charlie Brown* cartoons,
and several other cartoon series for television,

as well as narrations for documentaries, educational programs, and promotional materials.

He has also worked as a contributing writer for a Swedish music magazine.

In 1990, he moved to the USA. A few years later, he began working in the computer industry specializing in computer forensics, IT, and multimedia engineering.

This is Jakob Wahlberg's first book.

He can be reached via email at mindflossing@yahoo.com.

He currently resides in Waltham, Massachusetts.

Printed in the United States
45294LVS00007B/4-9

9 781425 903466